HEALING

SHIVANI AGRAWAL

*THIS BOOK IS DEDICATED TO MY OWN
FUTURE SELF.*

Contents

Contents

Hello everyone. I am Shivani Agrawal writing my 2nd book on poems.

The feelings, gratitude, emotions are expressed with writing my poems

in the form of free verse of rhyme scheme.

God has given ocean to explore, so why not dive in it?

Preface

Acknowledgements

THANKS TO MY MOTHER AND DAD FOR MOTIVATING ME...

1. LISTEN WHEN IT RAINS

Listen when is is pitter-pattering
As it hits the ground,
There are million secrets that come along.
Observe when it rains,
The clouds circle around the mountains
And stucks at the head of the tree.
Look around when it rains,
You will see million droplets of water,
Cuddling around like a little baby.
The baby water plays around with leaves,
Tress and the ground.
Listen when it rains,
Your heart will pound.

2. PAW PAW

You are always there for me,
Even if I am sad, drained, happy or tied up withing the walls.
You always sit beside me,
Like blowing air.
Whenever I cry,
You wipe down the tears for me.
I always like the way you move your tail.
The way you move your tail,
Matches with my heartbeat.
Empty spaces of my house
Are either covered by you or your hair.
Oh boy!
I know you steal my food.
But the way you look at me,
Through your glittery eyes
Always make me forgive you.
You will always be my little paw paw..

3. LIES

You left me with lies,
Leaving me behind and asking me why.
You and I both knew we were odd pairs,
But I didn't care.
You healed my wounds,
We shared our pasts, present and many other stories.
You held my hands when I was lost,
But your words made me feel unworthy.
Now every time you speak,
I start feeling scared.
Previously you made me feel like a princess,
Now I feel like a piece of used tissue.
I only have your memories,
But not the previous you.

4. HAPPINESS

Come here to the forest,
Where the time flies slow and memories are more.
Come here to the nature,
Where your mind relaxes and soul needs healing.
As sitting on the bench, I can hear the soulful chirping of birds.
I can smell the scent of grass,
The pleasant smell of each and every flower!
I can see the birds hopping like a baby,
On the green and yellow grass,
As they move forward to see the greenery.
Oh! Come here , to see the dragonflies,
Leaving their magical tails behind.
Look after the mountains ,
Which are standing still
And giving us the mixture of beauty and happiness we need..

5. AIR CRAFT

Blistering rays of the sun,
Forms an image,
Of the beautiful and sparky, shiny
Cotton balls in the middle of retina.
It seems like a castle with some rivers and mountains alongside.
Rays beautifully and parallel falling on the hands of passengers.
Seeming like a sea carrying number of passengers,
Some knowing their destiny
While others are going to create their destiny.
The way they will be going,
Will be making entire difference in their life.

6. CUTE LITTLE MONSTER

I made a castle in the air of you,
To be the flower of my life.
The rainbow to blow up on the clouds,
Rain to shower happiness in my life,
Butterfly to draw beautiful patterns in the cloud
Colours that would splash on the walls beautifully.
I dreamed you to be the beautiful patterns in the cloud,
I thought to draw our beautiful painting.
But rather you became the thorny devil flower in my life,
Dark patchy colours that would haunt me day and night,
Acid rains that burn my body,
And the patterns that terrify me.
Thank you, my cute little devil,
Yet beautifully formed mind!

7. DEAR ME IN 10 YEARS

Dear me in ten years. I'll make you damn proud of yourself
We'll believe in ourselves and fight against the world.
We'll face every problem with courage and be strong in each and every
situation
Dear me in 10 years, we'll make our younger self happy and proud of
what we will become.
Dear me in 10 years, you will be making your parents satisfied with you.
You'll get to know about people, world and so many other things.
After sometime you'll understand that nothing is permanent, everyone
will go and vanish one day.
There is one quote 'people can go from people you know to people you
don't'.
Don't worry about the people focus on yourself...
We will do hard work and remove all the negativities from our life.
The problems that you had faced will teach you something
Your younger self will work very hard to make you climb through the
stairs of life.
Your younger self will not quit because of the challenges of life.
Dear me in 10 years, you're worthy and I'm proud of you.

8. FLOWER

Once there was a flower,
Prettiest of all,
Loved by her owner,
Stood bravely in the scorching heat of sun,
Still blooming with all her heart.
Had supportive soil,
That provided her with nutrients and support.
She was the bravest of all,
In spite of her dark days.
But one day ,
She lost her hope and gave up on living.
As she was disturbed by the destructive rain and thunderstorm.
Little she could think,
Was only of her happy days.
How she used to bloom and dance with the wind
How beautiful those moments were with her owner.
How many enjoyful days she has with the soil.
Thinking of these things made her anxious.
During those dark days,
She thought of the people and things that loved her,
Took care of her.
Made her feel worthy and motivated every day.
Little by little,
She made her stronger by understanding these situations,

Lots of people loved her and wanted her to bloom forever.
She decided to restart her life,
To live for her own self
And lead a new, happy, stronger life again.

9. GAME

Let's play something, shall we?
After that don't you dare to plead.
We've seen people and ourselves being hurt
Now it's the time of ours to be shut.
Let's just be opposite,
So that we can see the world from different objectives.
When I'll be hurt, you'll be happy.
When I'll laugh, you'll cry.
When I'll speak, you'll keep your mouth stitched,
So don't you dare to keep your mind glitched.
Either we'll both go completely mad or kill ourselves.
As we'll become powerless.
Do you dare to play this game? Are you in?

10. QUEEN

She's a girl, they say.
Can't do this or that or pay her bills
They say she's frightened by the world
But can't accept they should be the only one referred.
Cook and clean are the only works,
Because of this the condition gets worse.
But she's the girl who is the creator of this world,
And should be left undisturbed.
She's the one who is independent,
Serves nature as a present.
She's the one who beats,
Whenever her own self is in need.
Women have crown,
And there is no one that can make them feel down

11. SUPERHERO

You have a heart as big as an ocean,
And you don't show how soft you are from inside often
You never showed a drop of tear,
As you were busy to wipe our tears my dear.
You carry responsibilities like a soldier,
But you have so many responsibilities and problems on your shoulders.
When someone ask your problems,
You mop it with a smile
But nobody understands your small inner child.
You too, often want shoulders to cry on
But your burden stops doing it from.
You ignore your needs and dreams to fulfil your child needs.
I, someday want to become like you
And I am so proud of you.
I love you papa!

12. PRINCESS

Remember. Remember
To love yourself day and night
You're beautiful, you're beautiful.
No matter how dark the days you face,
You'll be the one in race
You're beautiful, you're beautiful.
Previously you're the one who was lost,
But you're the one who changed the plot
You're beautiful, you're beautiful.
Don't you think you've lost the war,
Remember what you are for
You're beautiful, you're beautiful.
Don't you feel low..
Na... Na... Na..
I won't let you do that,
Na. Naa. Naa.
You're beautiful, you're beautiful!!

13. BLACK AND WHITE

When I was five,
I used to tell my mother to read fables and rhymes.
Saw the world colourful,
And thought everything was beautiful.
When I got ten,
I learned how to hold a pen.
Started to see some parts of the world black and white,
Because I didn't think everything was going right.
When I got fifteen,
I saw everyone mean.
Saw the dark side of the world,
And got to know no one leaves you undisturbed.
They call you the worst,
And hurt with their words.
This is the cycle of the world, my dear
That everyone has to face..

14. FRIENDSHIP

My definition of friendship is kind of weird,
Because it can break you in tears.
'Friend' they used to say,
At the end heart is the thing with which they play.
Forever they used to call,
But you'll be the one who'll get small.
I used to shed rains for them,
But I didn't know that they will be the reason of the dark clouds.
I was scared to lose them, it was a fear
Now I don't even want them in near.
I don't know if I could ever find a true friend,
But if I'll find, I'll be sure it will soon end...

15. STRONG

Oh boy! There's a story of a girl,
Who was so strong n courageous.
Something came up and broke her trust,
Used to lock herself in the rooms and burst.
The small diamonds were accompanied by scream and shout,
And was afraid of every single thing around.
Everything seemed to be a monster for her,
But she kept record per.
The tears she stored and the screams that echoed,
Were like a misfortune for her
But she accepted everything like a father's daughter.
Built tear as stairs and scream as an energy,
To move forward and look everything expertly.
Please my girl be like this,
Because everyone wants your bliss..

16. MAGIC

Mirror, mirror..
Tell me what you see in the deep sparkly eyes,
Of the people who lies.
Mirror, mirror.
Is there another parallel world behind you?
Where the fairies dance and leave their trail behind..
Mirror , mirror..
Do you have a secret port?
Where the moon hangs with a string,
And the stars flow magically on a river, clinging.
Mirror, mirror..
Do you have a shimmery lake,
Where the swans and the fishes play.

17. STREET DOG

Where are you humans?
Am I not sufficient for your love?
Just because I live in streets
You roll me down like a sheet
You regard me as a dirty thing,
And don't bring me anything.
I hop around the corners with one leg,
Because of your applied breaks.
Searching for food, I cry
But you don't even try to give me a bite.
Rolling like a dry leaf I wander
Whether my existence even touched you, my dear.

18. LAST TIME

Last time when we met
We cried so much that our eyes got red.
We were so happy to see each other,
That the world around us didn't bother.
Fairies met and oceans separated
From different worlds, we created .
Words were less,
To say the things we wanted to express.
Eyes spoke louder than our mouths
Of the things we wanted to say out loud.
Last time when we met
We got distant,
And let the oceans forget

19. CANDLES

Merry, a girl, goes round n round
The beautiful garden with her pinkish frock around.
Plays around with her friends in the mud,
And all the happiness within her floods.
Dances in the rain with group
With all her joy in loop.
Her birthday came once,
In which she invited all her beloved ones.
With every candles she blew,
Her age started to grew.
Until one day she realised
These were only the memories she memorized..

20. DREAM

Child, wake up.

I heard a noise,

Which was unusual than ever.

When I woke up I was at an unrevealed place,

At the corner where the music was selcouth.

Zephyr wind was blowing which caused eunoia.

Small birds were telling jokes which happened to be jayus,

And I couldn't stop but be infatuated with that place.

Aurora was at it's peak,

That caused a pleasing environment.

Small butterflies wandered around that left a trail of magic behind,

Swans danced and flew with their hands tied.

Clouds were a bunch of cotton balls,

And waterfalls glitter.

But I was awoke as the reality of life stroked my head..

21. MY LITTLE LIFE

Writing in one corner of the room
Unaware of the fact that something would happen with me
Around me flowers and petals bloom.
My father bought a little puppo,
Which was furry and adorable.
Wrapped around my arms, it cuddled
Like a little baby in my wing, I giggle.
I couldn't stop but look at that 'little life',
To ease my sadness and stay alive.
Hopping like a grasshopper it walked,
With it's small paws which had delightfulness locked.
Eventually with the time that 'little life' got bigger,
And my life with it shimmered...

22. RESILIENCE RISING

I knew that I was enough,
When everything was going rough.
People around me changed
Like they never happened to me in my life.
Petals scorched and water dried,
I had nothing in my hands but I tried.
I came forward as a warrior,
Who fought every war rigorously
And tackled every problem as a leader.
It's the new life for me,
Which changed
And the new
Developed human is uncaged.

23. CHILDHOOD MEMORIES

My mother tells me,
Of all the things that had happened to me.
Its blurry but I still remember
How innocent we used to be.
Playing in the sand and building blocks
Were only the things we worried about.
We weren't double faced
Or were in a race.
I still remember
How beautiful were those moments
When we used to be friends without greediness.
Please God,
Take me to the past
Where the time flies slow,
And the memories are more.

24. WHO AM I?

Who am I?
Am I some kind of toy to be played around?
Or a piece of used tissue to be thrown on the ground?
Who am I? You ask
I'm the laughter that fills the room with joy
I'm the sunshine of everyone's life.
I'm not the colour of the skin or the clothes I wear
I'm the person who I am
I'm a healing poetry,
And I'm the mirror which shows reality.

25. GROW

When did we grow from,
Crying about the wounds
To actually hurting ourselves
When did we grow from,
Being afraid of the snakes
To actually be one of them
When did we grow from
Being different from each other
To walking in the same path
When did we grow from
Having a playful mind
To have depressive battles each week
When did we grow from
Crying Infront of everyone
To locking up ourselves in the washroom
When did our actual smiles
Get converted into fake ones
When did we grow from
Learning alphabets
To actually writing about our problems?

26. SMILE

Zephyr wind blowing and hearing the roaring of the sea,
Causes aviothic feeling that cannot be left unseen.
I love collecting the shells! She exclaimed
And everyday collected one shell as a present.
Each shell made her feel better,
And escaped her from the things that would happen later.
She was happy as a clam,
And the pearl of the shell made her feel enlightened.
The shells which she collected were a charm,
As they were the smile of the sea till last as her calm..

27. OCEAN BEAUTY

Coming from the depth of the sea
I can see a wild, medium creature coming near me.
The blue shimmery reflection of the blue monster
Making the effect of the creature more appreciable.
Wearing droplets of sea water as an ornament
And a crown made up of the beauty of the ocean.
Fairies of the sunlight danced
And the scent of the ocean moved on.
It was not an ordinary creature,
But a beauty of nature
To be remarked..

28. COLOURFUL SKIES

In this actuality of the shattered series,
Preserved souls of worn-out feelings live.
When die,
Goes to the sky
And enters the magical world of fairies lie.
Colourful skies and phenomenal view
Gets the heart of very few.
You know but you don't
That these skies
Are the hearts of the people who admires every single star...

29. RECOGNIZE

Gathered with all the souls along with happiness,
And alot of fun which is never less.
The colourless heart is filled with rainbows
With a pinch of naughtiness along.
The dry trees and alive again,
And the joyful years are regained.
With this a new person will arise,
With clever mind and beautiful heart
Which could never be recognized..

30. LAST CALL

My heart's filled with joy,
Whenever I talk to you.
Your smile, voice keep me awaken
Through day and night.
Whenever I look at you, I get afraid
Whether it's our first call.
Whether the next day,
I would open the door of a parallel world
Whether there would be another day for me.
But still, I talk the way,
Whether it's our first call
Still the same shyness,
Happiness and joy.
I pray that whenever our first call takes place
I remind you that,
" You'll always be my loveliest being and no one can take your place ".

31. ONE OF US IS DEAD

Group of friends playing truth n dare,
Asked questions and gave tasks in pair.
Never thought this moment will come along
Enjoyed the most of their lives
Didn't know they had to give price.
They realized one of their friends was silent,
Asked if everything was alright.
Until one question popped up him,
" What if you were dead? "
Whole group went silent,
But waited for the answer with patience.
The boy answered with side smile,
I already am.
When the whole lights went off.
The group shivered with horror,
Their hearts from their ribcage popped up.
They heard a scream which was of one of the members
Until the lights came and they were covered with terror.
The guy was vanished
And the other was killed.
His eyes were smashed and hearts out
The atmosphere was filled with terror.
Until they realised the doors were closed and windows shut,
And they were stuck there forever.

32. FLOWER

Blowing with the wind and dancing along with it,
Never ever thought this moment will come around.
It was loved by its owner
Watered daily, talked and took care of.
Now it was left alone
Undisturbed at one corner with no soil and water.
Until one day the owner saw it
But it was totally dried up.
And spoke
" I might not be your favourite but I loved you till my last breath "..

33. BEAUTIFUL TOO

Roses don't regard themselves as ugly,
Even though they have thorns, my honey.
You're beautiful just as they way you are
Even you've scars.
The sun rays falling straight on your face
Separates you from the race.
Rays are like a jewellery of your features
And nobody can even deny it either.
Your body is perfect
But it cannot be as same as others like you expect.
Every is different and beautiful
And see the world from their own objective, colourful..

34. RED ROSE

If time was meant to be a colour, you would be my golden hour.
If love was meant to be o be a seed, you would be my flower every day.
Sparkling eyes holding thousands of secrets,
Reveals when it comes to me.
I couldn't stop but gaze into your eyes,
Like I'm lost in some of my favourite memory.
Each day I feel that you're destined to me.
Your voice, hair everything is captured in my memories like a picture.
It never feels that I'm wasting time with you,
But spending each and every moment in happiness..

35. LOVELY

You don't know, how lovely you are.
Until those glittery blistering rays of the sun, touches your face and
making it special like no other one.
Your deep brownish eyes, holding millions of lies
That are uncovered whenever you come near me.
Oh! The way you touch your shiny hair,
That blows with the soft air
Touches my heart
And creates an art
That nobody's gonna set apart...

36. HUG

I want to hug someone so tight
That everything feels right.
I want to forget every problem of mine
And forever shine.
I want to cry out loud on the shoulders of someone
And tell them what has happened to me one on one.
I want someone who can hug me and tell me everything's going to be
okay,
And make one magical spray.
I want to hear
" You're not messed up for anything "
" You're worth everything "

37. READY TO START

Let's take a oath to try,
Because we cry.
We've got so many experiences,
Because this life is full of secrets.
Now we have to start,
Because crying is not a part.
I'm capable of doing everything,
Because I got to know world's meaning.
I'm sure this roller coaster would be fun,
And glow as a beautiful rising sun.
Let's pack out our feelings and emotions,
Because it would be worth it to remove salt from the ocean..

38. MAGICIAN

Maria has an outing with an magician,
And thought she was in a world of fiction.
"Hey! ", she exclaimed,
And the magician replied with his hands, stained.
They went to a fair,
Where everything got stopped and disappeared.
She got surprised,
And he bought her a teddy bear
Which was maximized.
She didn't believe
But the world from the boundaries around her release.
But she didn't know why she was feeling uncomfortable,
When he got vanished
And the next day she got to see
That the fair was diminished..

39. INCOMPLETE PUZZLE

Making the puzzle,

I still remember how excited i was

And broke all the time laws.

It was a great picture of mine with a wide smile,

That was quite a while.

Pieces by pieces I made that picture,

And it was a great achievement to achieve during leisure.

I don't know,

But I lost one piece

But no one believed.

It was the piece of my smile

That I lost

And paid a great cost...

40. PSYCHO

Dad see how beautiful is that butterfly,
I want to have it.
Dad see how beautiful it's wings are,
I want to touch it.
Dad I want that butterfly,
So that I can trap it.
Dad I want that butterfly,
So that it can flap it's wings in a certain area.
Dad I want that butterfly,
So that I can see her suffering.
Dad I want that butterfly,
So that she can die in her own blood in that beautiful cage..

41. CASTLE

I made a castle in the air of you to be the flower of my life,
The rainbow to blow up on the clouds,
Rain to shower happiness in my life,
The butterfly to draw beautiful patterns in the cloud,
Colours that would splash on the walls beautifully,
I castled you to be the beautiful patterns of the cloud,
I thought to drew our beautiful painting.
But rather you became the thorny demon flower in my life,
Dark patchy colours that would haunt me day and night,
Acid rain which burns my body,
And the patterns which terrify me.
Thank you my little devil yet well-formed mind!

www.ingramcontent.com/pod-product-compliance
Lightning Source LLC
Chambersburg PA
CBHW031513150726
47990CB00007B/3001